Library of Congress Cataloging in Publication Data

Sheehan, Angela.
    The bumblebee.

    (A first look at nature)
    Illustrations by M. Pledger.
    SUMMARY: Describes the life cycle and natural
environment of the bumblebee.
    1. Bumblebees—Juvenile literature. (1. Bumblebees)
I. Pledger, Maurice. II. Title.
QL568.A6S53   595.7'99   76-45486
ISBN 0-531-09078-7
ISBN 0-531-09053-1 lib. bdg.

Published by Warwick Press, 730 Fifth Avenue, New York, New York 10019
First published in Great Britain by Angus and Robertson in 1976
Copyright © 1976 by Grisewood & Dempsey Ltd.
Printed and Bound by Mandarin Publishers Ltd., Hong Kong
6 5 4 3 2 1

The Bumblebee

By Angela Sheehan
Illustrated by Maurice Pledger

WARWICK PRESS · NEW YORK

Each day the sun became warmer. The birds woke earlier and earlier. They sang for joy that winter had passed. The bumblebee queen had slept all winter in a tiny hole under a stone. Now she crawled from her snug hiding place and she felt very weak. She had had no food for more than six months.

Stretching her wings, she flew to a pussy willow nearby. Its flowers were covered with rich, yellow pollen. The queen bee settled down to her first meal, of pollen and sweet-tasting nectar.

For the next few weeks, the queen bee fed herself and bathed in the warm sunshine. At night she hid under stones or fallen leaves. Then it was time to build a nest.

At the foot of a wall that ran by the farm, the queen bee found a small hole. The hole had once been the home of a field mouse. She crawled in.

Deep inside there was dry grass and leaves. It was a perfect place to lay the eggs that were growing inside her.

Inside the hole, the queen bee made a little cell, shaped like a cup. She made it with wax. The wax came from the pollen she had eaten.

Next, the queen flew off to gather nectar and pollen. When she came back she put some into the cell. Then she pushed her tail into the cell and laid her first batch of eggs. There were ten in all. She made a lid of wax to cover the eggs and keep them safe. The nectar and pollen inside the cell would be food for the "worm-like" grubs when they hatched.

The queen, too, needed a store of food. So she made another little cell. She collected more nectar and filled the cell with it. On rainy days, when she could not go out, the queen fed from this "honey-pot".

It was important for the queen to keep her eggs warm. For five days she clung to the outside of the wax cell. Her furry body was like a thick blanket.

After five days, the eggs hatched into
little wriggling grubs. They soon finished
all the food in their cell. So the queen bit
through the wax and fed them through
the hole.

The grubs grew bigger and bigger. In
about two weeks they were fully grown.
Then each grub spun a thread of silk.
Turning round and round, they wrapped
the silk around their bodies. Soon they had
each made a soft cover of silk, called a
cocoon.

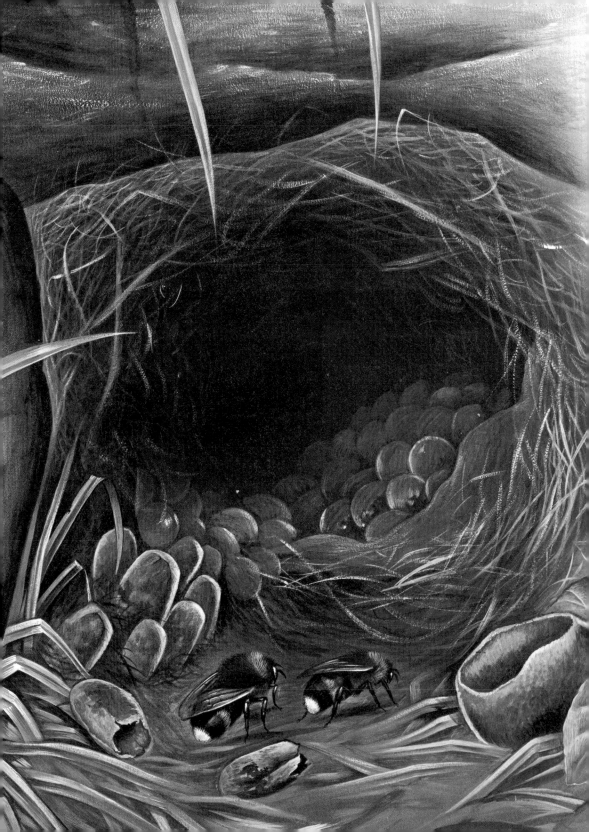

The queen bee carefully removed the old cell from around the cocoons. She used the wax to help make new cells, ready for more eggs.

Inside the cocoons, the little white grubs were slowly turning into bees. After two weeks the young bees pushed their way out of the silky cocoons. Their wings were wet and they could not fly.

The queen had to find food for the young bees. This was easy when the sun was shining. But for two days it did not stop raining. The queen could not go out, so she had to use the nectar in the honey-pot.

The wings of the young bees soon dried and they grew stronger and stronger. Now they could start work. The bees were all female workers. They had to help their mother make new cells and raise the other grubs. As fast as new cells were made, the queen filled them with eggs.

Some of the workers stayed in the nest to feed the grubs. Others went out to collect more pollen and nectar. Every day there were more and more grubs to feed in the cells. And each time a batch of cocoons burst open, there were eight, ten, or even fourteen new worker bees.

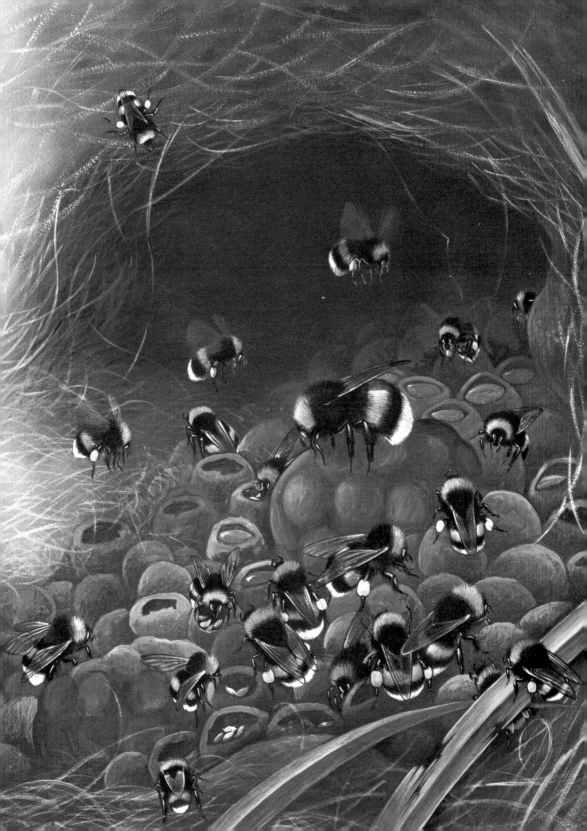

After a few months, the nest was
really crowded. There were more than a
hundred bees. The workers had to add new
walls of dry grass to the front of the
nest to make more room.

Now the fields and woods were full
of flowers. At the farm there was clover.
In the hedges there was bindweed and
deadnettle. And foxgloves grew by the wood.

The workers gathered food from
these flowers. But they still needed
more. Each day they flew farther and
farther. Sometimes they flew so far
that they could not reach home by
nightfall. Then they had to find a
hiding place until morning. One bee
even went to sleep curled up in a
foxglove flower. She was still tired
at dawn, and her fur was wet with dew.

She arrived home just as the other workers were leaving to find flowers. As they buzzed out of the nest, they flew straight into a young badger. The nocturnal badger should really have been home in bed by this time, but it could smell honey.

It was clawing at the door of the nest when the bees inside felt its hot breath.

The angry bees flew out to attack the badger. Crowding around, they stung it on the nose again and again. Instead of a tasty meal of bumblebees and honey, the badger fled with a sore nose.

If the badger's mother had attacked the nest, it would have been different. Her tough nose could stand a few stings.

Although the nest was well hidden, the bees had to make sure that no other enemies attacked them. One of their enemies was very sly. It was a cuckoo bee. The cuckoo bee lays its eggs in a bumblebee's nest. Once inside the nest, it hides until it smells like all the other bees and none of them notices it. Then it kills the queen and lays its own eggs in her cells. When the eggs hatch the bumblebee workers feed the grubs. They do not know that they are looking after their enemy's young.

One day a cuckoo bee did creep up on the nest. The workers were too busy to see it. It was right inside before they knew what had happened. The angry bees began to buzz. They left their jobs and rushed towards the invader. The cuckoo bee hit out with its stinger and the first workers fell back, dead. But soon more bees arrived. In the end their stingers pierced the cuckoo bee's armor and it lay dead. Its young would never be born. The bees were safe.

Toward the end of the summer, the queen laid fewer eggs. There were now so many workers to look after them and feed them that the last grubs grew very big indeed. When they broke out of their cocoons, they would be queen bees like their mother.

At the same time, too, the first male bees wriggled from their cocoons. Male bees are called drones. Drones are very lazy. They do no work at all.

But there was not much work to do now, anyhow. The summer days grew shorter and the flowers began to die. The workers grew too tired to go out to get food. As the flowers died, they died too.

The queen was old now. In one summer, she had raised more than a hundred workers and twelve fine young queen bees. Her work was done. One evening she left the nest. She settled sleepily on a flower and, as the sun sank, she fell into a deep sleep and died.

Within a few days, almost all the
workers were dead. Only the young
queens and drones were strong and
healthy. They also had to leave the nest.
The drones left first, on their first flight.

They did not go far from the nest
because they wanted to mate with the
young queens. The queens, too, felt the
need to find a mate. So they flew from the
nest high into the air.

As the queens flew, the drones followed them. Some queens were caught by drones from their own nest; others by drones from another nest. One young queen flew high over the wood. She was followed closely by one of the drones. As she grew tired, he clutched her in the air and they mated. A moment later the drone fell from the sky. He was dead.

Like all the other drones, he had flown only once. But in that flight he had made it possible for a whole nest of bees to be born next summer.

Once she had mated, the young queen flew on. In spring she would have to build a nest for her own eggs, as her mother had done.

There would be no food for the new queen in the winter and the weather would be cruel and cold. She must quickly find a place to shelter.

The new queen fed on the last of the
summer flowers and her body grew fat.
The autumn leaves fell, making a brown
carpet on the woodland floor. Then the
queen bee crawled under some leaves and
slowly went to sleep.

It would be more than six months before
she woke. Rain, snow, and hail would fall.
But she would be warm and safe in her
winter bed.

More About Bumblebees

Where to see Bumblebees

Bumblebees are found all over the world. There are many different kinds. Each kind has its own pattern of stripes and colors. Some are big, like the one in the story. Others are smaller. During the summer you can see worker bees almost anywhere, if there are flowers nearby.

Food from Flowers

If there were no flowers, there would be no bumblebees. For bumblebees eat only nectar and pollen. They have good eyes and can find brightly colored flowers easily. When a bumblebee settles on a flower, it sucks up nectar with its tongue. The tongue is a hollow tube.

The bumblebee does not use up all the nectar it sucks up. It stores some inside its body and brings it back for the young bees to eat. The nectar is changed into honey. It is stored in honey-pots in the nest.

Baskets of Pollen

As well as nectar, bumblebees collect and eat pollen. If you look closely at a bumblebee's back legs you will often see balls of yellow pollen clinging to them. The pollen is stuck to rows of stiff hairs that grow down each side of the legs. The hairs make a kind of basket. As the bee feeds, pollen is brushed off the flower on to its furry body. The bee then combs the pollen off its back on to its legs. When it reaches home, the bee sweeps the pollen from the basket into cells. So there is always a good store.

As a bee lands on a flower, it may brush on to it some of the pollen gathered from the

worker

queen

drone

The three kinds of bumblebee

one before. This is good for the flower. It needs the pollen from another flower to make its seeds. So the flowers need the bees as much as the bees need the flowers.

Wax Works

The queen bee and the workers make cells for the nest with wax. Some of the pollen the bees swallow turns into wax inside their bodies. The bee squeezes out the wax. Then she shapes the wax into cells.

Sting in the Tail

Everyone knows that bees sting. But they only use their stingers if they think they are in danger. The stinger is a tiny tube in the bee's tail. The bee pierces its enemy's skin with the sharp point and then squirts poison through it.

Honeybees have stingers with little points called barbs down the sides. When they use their stinger, it sometimes gets caught in their victim's skin. It cannot be pulled out again. The bee has to leave its stinger behind when it flies off. So it can only sting once. Bumblebee stingers have no barbs, so they can sting again and again.

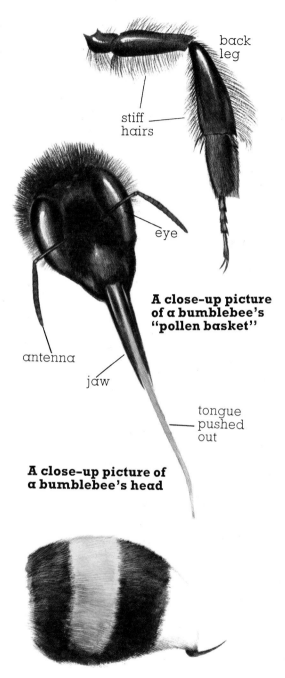

back leg

stiff hairs

eye

A close-up picture of a bumblebee's "pollen basket"

antenna

jaw

tongue pushed out

A close-up picture of a bumblebee's head

A bumblebee's stinger